BIOGRAPHY FROM

ANCIENT CIVILIZATIONS

LEGENDS, FOLKLORE, AND STORIES OF ANCIENT WORLDS

The Life and Times of
Attila the Hun

Mitchell Lane
PUBLISHERS
P.O. Box 196
Hockessin, Delaware 19707
www.mitchelllane.com

TITLES IN THE SERIES

The Life and Times of

BIOGRAPHY FROM
ANCIENT CIVILIZATIONS
LEGENDS, FOLKLORE, AND STORIES OF ANCIENT WORLDS

The Life and Times of

Attila the Hun

Earle Rice Jr.

PUBLISHERS

Printing   1   2   3   4   5   6   7   8   9

Library of Congress Cataloging-in-Publication Data
Rice, Earle.
  The life and times of Attila the Hun / by Earle Rice Jr.
    p. cm.—(Biography from ancient civilizations) (The life and times of)
  Includes bibliographical references and index.
  ISBN 978-1-58415-741-0 (library bound)
  1. Attila, d. 453—Juvenile literature. 2. Huns—Biography—Juvenile literature. 3. Huns—History—Juvenile literature. 4. Nomads—Asia, Central—History—Juvenile literature. 5. Nomads—Europe—History—Juvenile literature. 6. Asia, Central—History—Juvenile literature. 7. Europe—History—To 476—Juvenile literature. I. Title.
  D141.R535 2010
  936'.03092—dc22
  [B]
                                                            2009027362

ABOUT THE AUTHOR: Earle Rice Jr. is a former senior design engineer and technical writer in the aerospace, electronic-defense, and nuclear industries. He has devoted full time to his writing since 1993 and is the author of more than fifty published books. Earle is listed in *Who's Who in America* and is a member of the Society of Children's Book Writers and Illustrators, the League of World War I Aviation Historians, the Air Force Association, and the Disabled American Veterans.

PUBLISHER'S NOTE: This story is based on the author's extensive research, which he believes to be accurate. Documentation of such research is contained on page 46.

The internet sites referenced herein were active as of the publication date. Due to the fleeting nature of some web sites, we cannot guarantee they will all be active when you are reading this book.

To reflect current usage, we have chosen to use the secular era designations BCE ("before the common era") and CE ("of the common era") instead of the traditional designations BC ("before Christ") and AD (*anno Domini*, "in the year of the Lord").

BIOGRAPHY FROM
ANCIENT CIVILIZATIONS
LEGENDS, FOLKLORE, AND STORIES OF ANCIENT WORLDS

CONTENTS

*For Your Information

Nineteenth-century Hungarian painter Mór Than's *Feast of Attila* (detail) depicts the Hun chieftain on his throne, presiding over a banquet given in honor of emissaries from Eastern Roman emperor Theodosius II. The artist based his painting on the writings of Greek historian Priscus, who is on the right holding his history.

CHAPTER

ONE

THE RISE OF THE HUNS

In the last days of antiquity, the Huns set the standard for barbarians. They came from the east in the second half of the fourth century. They came from far beyond the Volga River that winds from the hills of Tver' Oblast in south Russia to the salt waters of the Caspian Sea between Europe and Asia. They thundered toward the Danube River on the backs of Turkish ponies bred to the extremes of the treeless grasslands of southern Asia known as the Steppes. Tales of terror raced ahead of them in their westward advance. Death and destruction lay behind them. The Huns—whose true origins no one knows for sure—reached the gates of Europe about the year 370 CE.

Popular belief often links the Huns with members of the Germanic race. Although they assimilated German-speaking tribes into their own ranks, the Huns themselves sprang from a breed apart. Many scholars believe the Huns descended from the Xiongnu (shee-OONG-noo). The Xiongnu (the old spelling, Hsiung-nu, is derived from the Chinese word *Hungnu*, for "barbarian") were a Turkic people that menaced China as early as the fifth century BCE. Qin Shi Huangdi, China's first emperor, built part of the Great Wall to keep them out.

According to historian and travel writer John Man, "The Xiongnu originally lived in the great northern loop of the Yellow River, in the area known today as the Ordos, in the Chinese province of Inner Mongolia."[1] Basically a nomadic people, they expanded their homelands to include parts of Manchuria and Siberia. Their economy depended largely on raising cattle and horses used for war or transport. They supplemented their roving existence by raiding other tribes. Fierce mounted Xiongnu warriors continued to terrorize their Chinese neighbors for centuries.

In the first century CE, the Xiongnu split into northern and southern branches. The southerners integrated into the Chinese culture under the Han dynasty. Their northern counterparts continued to pursue their independence in Mongolia. They soon began to drift westward in search of pristine pastures and new sources of wealth. By the middle of the second century CE, the northern Xiongnu had disappeared in the void of Central Asia.

Some two hundred years later, a tribe with a similar nomadic lifestyle emerged on the far-western end of Central Asia. Westerners soon began to call them Huns, perhaps from the Chinese word *Hungnu*, for they were certainly barbarians. And perhaps because of the short interval between the disappearance of the Xiongnu in Central Asia and the arrival of the Huns in Europe, Westerners—without solid proof—linked the two together.

Of the Huns' rude arrival in Europe, Ammianus Marcellinus, the last major Roman historian, wrote: "[A] hitherto unknown race of men had appeared from some remote corner of the earth, uprooting and destroying everything in its path like a whirlwind descending from high mountains."[2] The brief period of their appearance and subsequent disappearance lasted little more than a century.

Because the Huns did not write, they left no written accounts of their own history. All original source material about the Huns was penned by outsiders. Few of these early chroniclers spoke Hunnish; even fewer knew the Huns firsthand. Most were either enemies or victims of the Huns. Not surprisingly, they portrayed the Huns only at their worst. St. Jerome, a scholarly priest living in Bethlehem, described the marauding Huns as they swept across Asia Minor late in the fourth century:

> They filled the whole earth with slaughter and panic as they
> flitted hither and thither on their swift horses. They were at hand
> everywhere before they were expected. By their speed they
> outstripped rumour, and they took pity neither upon religion nor

rank nor age nor wailing childhood. Those who had just begun to live found themselves facing death and, in ignorance of their plight, would smile amid the drawn swords of the enemy.[3]

In addition to the writings of Ammianus and St. Jerome, the works of the Greek historian Priscus and the untutored Goth historian Jordanes make up the bulk of contemporary accounts about the Huns. In the late 1700s, Edward Gibbon drew on such historical sources and gave the Huns a dramatic role in his classic account of *The Decline and Fall of the Roman*

The Huns crossed into Europe from the Steppes of Central Asia in 370 CE. In this early drawing, the illustrator depicts a Hun chieftain, perhaps Attila himself, seeking directions from a local traveler with a walking staff.

Empire. Still later, during World War I, British propagandists began to call the Germans "Huns" to characterize them as barbarians and arouse public hatred toward their enemy. The misuse of their name by the British—though historically inaccurate—forever linked the Huns with the Germans.

On their westward sweep across the Asian grasslands, the Huns easily overcame the Alans (or Alani). The Alans were members of the Sarmatians, a loose confederation of Iranian people. They inhabited the plains between the Volga and Don rivers. Though fierce fighters, the Alans proved no match for the mounted archers of the Huns. In *The Decline*, Gibbons described the demise of the Alans: "On the banks of the Tanais [old name for the Don] the military power of the Huns and the Alani encountered each other with equal valour, but with unequal success. The Huns prevailed in the bloody contest; the king of the Alani was slain; and the remains of the vanquished nation were dispersed by the ordinary alternative of flight or submission."[4] Some of the defeated Alan warriors joined ranks with their conquerors. The Huns continued to move west, stronger than ever.

Shortly after 370 CE, the Huns clashed with the Ostrogoths. The Ostrogoths formed a part of a confederation of Germanic tribes known as the Goths. In the 300s, the Goths split into two groups—the Ostrogoths and the Visigoths. The Ostrogoths lived in the area of present-day Ukraine; the Visigoths, north of the lower Danube in Dacia (now in Romania). According to Jordanes, the Goths had originated in southern Scandinavia. The Huns, as they had with the Alans, quickly overran and absorbed the Ostrogoths. Next to feel the wrath of the growing Hunnic Empire were the Visigoths.

In 376, in a series of relentless attacks, the Huns drove the Visigoths southward across the Danube River into the Eastern Roman Empire. Roman officials allowed the fleeing Goths to enter the empire, but unkind treatment under the Romans soon provoked the fugitives to rebel. Their revolt led to the landmark triumph of barbarian cavalry over Roman foot soldiers at Adrianople (now Edirne, in European Turkey) in 378. By some estimates, the Visigoths—joined by Hun mercenaries, Ostrogoths, Alans, and other eastern nomads—annihilated as many as 40,000 legionnaires, including the Eastern Roman emperor, Valens.

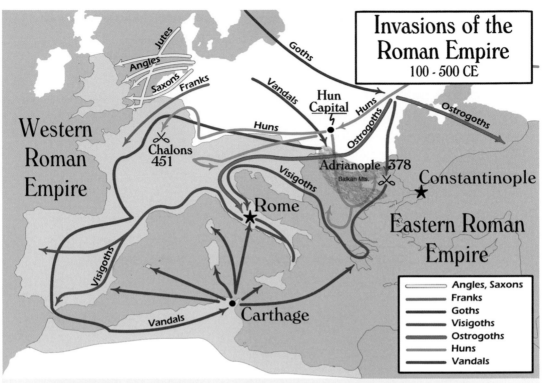

Invasions of the
Roman Empire
100 - 500 CE

Western
Roman
Empire

Jutes

Angles

Saxons

Franks

Chalons
451

Vandals

Huns

Goths

Hun
Capital

Huns

Ostrogoths

Ostrogoths

Visigoths

Adrianople 378
Balkan Mts.

Rome

Constantinople

Eastern Roman
Empire

Visigoths

Carthage

Vandals

	Angles, Saxons
	Franks
	Goths
	Visigoths
	Ostrogoths
	Huns
	Vandals

Beyond the reach of Rome and Constantinople, barbarians roamed the broad expanses of Western Europe during the 4th and 5th centuries. After the fall of Rome in 476 CE, nomadic tribes began to take root and build the nations that form the map of today's Europe.

Following the massive defeat of the Romans, the Huns unleashed their hordes of horrific horsemen not only in the Balkans but also southward into the rich lands of Syria. Everywhere they went, their warriors inspired fear. Their physical appearance alone was enough to start even the bravest heart thumping wildly. Writing about 395, Ammianus Marcellinus recorded perhaps the earliest detailed description of the Huns: "They have squat bodies, strong limbs, and thick necks, and are so prodigiously ugly and bent that they might be two-legged animals, or the figures crudely carved from stumps which are seen on the parapets of bridges."[5]

Despite his unflattering depiction of their appearance, Ammianus, a military man himself, seems to have admired the fighting qualities of the

Huns. Continuing, he wrote: "They sometimes fight by challenging their foes to single combat, but when they join battle they advance in packs, uttering their various war-cries. Being lightly equipped and very sudden in their movements they can deliberately scatter and gallop about at random, inflicting tremendous slaughter."[6]

In the half-century following their defeat of the Visigoths, the Huns established themselves as a major force in Europe. Despite their military successes, however, they lacked a single leader to establish a centralized authority. They operated as a loose confederation of tribes, answering to many chieftains or kings. Although a few "high kings" existed, none held the power or ability to control all of the Huns. They mostly operated and attacked under separate commands and without coordinated objectives.

In the second decade of the fifth century, leadership of the Huns narrowed to a "dual kingship" shared by two brothers, Octar (or Oktar) and Ruga (also Rua or Rugila). Octar died in 430, and Ruga emerged as the sole leader of the Hun Empire. Ruga forged an alliance with a Roman general named Flavius Aetius (FLAY-vee-us EE-tee-us). As a teenager, Aetius had been held hostage by the Huns and had become friendly with

them. Aided by Aetius, Ruga led the Huns on a campaign against the Germanic tribes in the Western Roman Empire. He later conducted numerous raids against the Eastern Romans.

In 434, Ruga was preparing for a massive invasion of the Eastern Roman Empire when—allegedly—a lightning bolt struck him dead. Ruga left a brother named Mundzuk (MOON-dyuk). Mundzuk had two sons named Bleda (BLAY-duh) and Attila (AT-uh-luh *or* uh-TIH-luh). They succeeded Ruga in another dual kingship. Bleda's name soon faded into history. Attila's name still resonates like a shriek of terror from out of the past.

Early Christians called Attila the "Scourge of God."

Battle of Adrianople

By the time the Huns had overrun the Visigothic kingdom in 376, the glory that was Rome had faded. Emperor Valens ruled the eastern part of the Roman Empire from Constantinople (Istanbul); his nephew Gratian, the western part from Rome. Valens permitted Goth fugitives from the Hun invasion to seek refuge in the Eastern Empire, but with conditions. He demanded that every Goth male under military age be given up as a hostage, and that all Goth weapons be handed over to Roman officials.

In 377, Valens marched against the Persians. He left two corrupt underlings in charge of collecting weapons from the Goths. His subordinates enriched themselves at Gothic expense. They accepted money and other favors in return for allowing the Goths to keep their weapons. Harsh Roman treatment and continual demands for bribes drove the Visigoths to revolt. They allied themselves with the Ostrogoths and other nomads and rampaged about the lands north of the Balkan mountains.

After months of heavy fighting, Roman forces at the Danube could not contain the Goths. Valens brought up his field army from the Euphrates region, while Gratian set out from the Rhine frontier with his forces. The summer of 378 found the Goths retreating toward the city of Adrianople (Edirne), about 130 miles west of Constantinople (see map on page 11). On July 9, 378, Valens marched out of Adrianople with about 40,000 infantry and 20,000 cavalry. Without waiting for Gratian's troops to arrive, Valens met and engaged the Goths at their camp some twelve miles north of the city.

Two things influenced his decision to go it alone: He did not respect the fighting qualities of the Goths; and he did not want to share what he thought would be an easy victory with his nephew. His reckless decision cost him his life and the lives of probably 40,000 of his legionnaires. After a Roman cavalry attack failed, the Gothic cavalry struck the Roman infantry on an exposed flank and cut them to pieces. The crushing defeat of the Romans at Adrianople established the supremacy of cavalry over infantry for the next thousand years.

A Gothic cavalryman

During Attila's twenty-year reign as king of the Huns, he maintained a base camp in central Hungary. Today's Hungary claims the Huns as one of its seven founding tribes. This statue honoring Attila stands at the Millennium Memorial in Budapest's Heroes Square.

CHAPTER
TWO

AND THEN THERE WAS ONE

Attila, in the words of Goth historian Jordancs, "was a lover of war yet restrained in action, mighty in counsel, gracious to supplicants [those seeking favors], and lenient to those once received under his protection."[1] The fearsome and many-sided king of the Huns who became known as the Scourge of God was born in 406. Other than the year of his birth, almost nothing is known of his early life. He was probably born somewhere in Pannonia (modern Hungary), but the Huns kept no records. "No one if asked can tell you where he comes from," wrote Roman historian Ammianus Marcellinus, "having been conceived in one place, born somewhere else, and reared even further off."[2] Attila's story essentially begins when he joined his elder brother Bleda as co-king of the Huns in 434.

Most scholars agree that Attila and Bleda shared a joint kingship. Some say that Attila served as his brother's second-in-command. In either case, the brothers split the kingdom between them. Bleda ruled in what is now Hungary. Attila held sway in the region farther down the Danube in present-day Romania. Over the century of its existence, the Hunnic Empire varied in its reach. At its peak, it stretched from the Central Asian steppes to deep into modern-day Germany, and from the Baltic Sea to the Black Sea. Its immensity owed much to the equally huge ambition of Mundzuk's youngest son.

Jordanes described Attila as a man who "was born to shake nations."[3] He paints this picture of the Hun ruler: "He was short of stature, with a broad chest and a large head; his eyes were small, his beard thin and sprinkled with gray; and he had a flat nose and a swarthy complexion, showing the evidences of his origin."[4] A story of the Sword of Mars—first recorded by the Greek historian Priscus and quoted a century later by Jordanes—illustrates the extent of Attila's aspirations:

A certain herdsman saw one of his heifers limping. Unable to find a cause for such a wound, he anxiously followed the trail of blood and at length came to a sword the beast had unwittingly trampled while grazing. He dug it up and straight away took it to Attila. He rejoiced at this gift and being of great courage he decided he had been appointed to be ruler of the whole world and that, thanks to the Sword of Mars, he had been granted the power to win wars.[5]

Huns attacking across an open plain struck fear in the hearts of even the bravest of their opponents. As cavalry, the Huns knew few equals and no superiors in their time.

Attila's means for becoming "ruler of the whole world" resided with tens of thousands of mounted archers. As if born to the backs of their horses, these barbarian cavaliers astounded Westerners with their horsemanship. The accuracy of their bronze- or iron-tipped arrows, let loose from composite bows at a gallop, further amazed all who opposed them. Their ferocious looks and piercing battle cries intimidated even the stoutest of foes that either gave way or fell before them. They lived in movable, round, tent-like shelters called yurts or gers. But they virtually ate, slept, negotiated, lived, loved, married, and died on the backs of their horses. One Roman scribe described them as savages spawned by witches, with lumps for heads and pinholes for eyes. Their enemies saw them as beings less than human and closer to low-legged beasts. Such were the instruments of Attila's quest for world dominion.

Before Attila and Bleda took control of the Huns, Ruga, their predecessor, had advanced his forces into Thrace in the Balkan Peninsula. Their presence there threatened the Eastern Roman Empire ruled by Emperor Theodosius II. Some historians of his day described Theodosius II as effeminate and cowardly. Rather than fight the Huns, he opted to buy peace. He agreed to pay an annual tribute of 350 pounds of gold to the Huns. When Ruga died, Theodosius II decided to end his agreement with the Huns. Attila and Bleda saw little to like in the emperor's decision. Bleda demanded a meeting with representatives of the Eastern Roman government. The fact that Bleda made the demand supports the claim that he ruled alone as king of the Huns with Attila only as his lieutenant.

In 435, Attila and Bleda met with Roman emissaries named Plinthas and Epigenes in Margus (now Požarevac in present-day Serbia). Margus, an important trade center, was located at the mouth of the Morava River where it joins the Danube. The Huns insisted on negotiating from the backs of their hardy, Steppe-bred ponies. In the Treaty of Margus, Plinthas authorized one Roman concession after another. He agreed to double the annual tribute paid to the Huns from 350 to 700 pounds of gold; to open Roman markets to Hunnish trade; to not enter into future alliances with enemies of the Huns or to void such existing alliances; to return escaped Roman prisoners or pay a ransom for each of one-ninth of a pound of gold (about $600 today); and to deny asylum to Hunnic defectors and return them at once. In return for these concessions, the Huns promised to keep the peace so long as the Romans kept the costly terms of the treaty.

After the one-sided negotiations, the Romans returned all fugitive Huns according to the terms of the treaty to show their good faith. Among them were two Hunnic princes, Mamas and Atakam, who had sought refuge with them. The Romans delivered them directly to Attila. As a warning to future defectors, Attila ordered the princes impaled on wooden stakes and mounted in view of the Romans. The skewered princes took two days to die. In the brutal times in which he lived, Attila clearly knew how to make a point.

Attila and Bleda returned to their home in the Great Plains of Hungary. Little is known of their activities for the next four years. Because their existence depended on war and its profits, they likely spent the years consolidating their forces and expanding their empire toward the Alps and the Rhine. Theodosius II used the time to shore up the walls of Constantinople, build the city's first seawall, and strengthen his border defenses along the Danube.

Beginning in 439, wars broke out on several fronts around the Roman Empire. In October of that year, the Vandals occupied Carthage, capital of Rome's holdings in North Africa. The Vandals were a Germanic tribe that invaded Gaul before settling in Spain. In 440, both parts of the empire sent forces to defend Sicily, ninety miles (145 kilometers) across the Mediterranean Sea from Carthage. While Roman forces were busy defending Sicily, the Sassanid Persians attacked the East Romans in Armenia in 441. Attila and Bleda resurfaced at this time to stir up more trouble for Theodosius II along the Danube.

In violation of the Treaty of Margus, the Huns laid waste to the Roman fortress at Constantia, across the river from Margus. They followed up with an attack on the nearby trade fair. Thereafter, the Huns thundered down upon Roman bastions (now in Serbia) in quick succession. Margus, Viminacium (Kostolac), Singidunum (Belgrade), and Sirmium (near Sremska Mitrovica) fell before their onslaught. After their latest rampage, the Huns appeared satisfied with their conquests for the moment.

By 442, the Vandals had returned to Spain with their spoils. Theodosius II recalled his forces from North Africa, and a lull fell over his empire. With his army back home, Theodosius felt strong enough to cut off payments to the Huns. Attila and Bleda did not take kindly to the emperor's decision. In 443, they stormed deep into the heart of the Eastern Roman Empire.

The Huns ravaged Naissus (modern Nis) and Serdica (Sofia, Bulgaria). Turning toward Constantinople, they left Philippolis (Plovdiv) and Arcadiopolis (Lüleburgaz) in ruins. In a series of clashes, they decimated the main East Roman forces. Onward they clattered, until they reached the sea north and south of Constantinople. Unable to breach the double walls of the Eastern capital, they wheeled back and crushed the remnants of the empire's forces in what is now the Gallipoli Peninsula.

Without an army, Theodosius II decided that it might be a good time to arrange another peace settlement with the Huns. He sent Consul-Senator Anatolius to negotiate a settlement. The First Peace of Anatolius

History springs to life in this hand-colored woodcut showing the Huns riding down on Moravia, now in the Czech Republic. Hunnish lances and flails, clearly seen here, cut a wide swath before the advancing Huns.

Huns generally preferred to fight at a distance using bow and arrows as their weapons of choice, but they sometimes used lassos to rope and thin out enemy formations. Up close, they wielded short swords and daggers with deadly efficiency.

granted the Huns 6,000 pounds of gold in unpaid tribute, trebled the annual tribute to 2,100 pounds of gold, and raised the gold ransom of each Roman prisoner by a third (about $800 today). Satisfied for the time being, the Huns again withdrew to their home base in the plains of Hungary.

Some time in 445, Attila either killed his brother Bleda or had him killed. Writing from the texts of Priscus, Jordanes alluded to Attila's likely reason: "Now when his brother Bleda, who ruled over a great part of the Huns, had been slain by his treachery, Attila united all the people under his own rule."[6] And then there was only one ruler of all the Huns.

Huns and Horses

In little more than a century, the Huns conquered part of Asia and half of Europe. From 350 to 470 CE, they terrorized the timid and slaughtered the bold across two continents. Their conquests came on the backs of small horses with large, long heads, big eyes, and short legs with broad hooves. The horse was their vehicle, their enabler, their way of life. Hun and horse together represented the finest and fastest light cavalry of their era.

A Hun infant could ride almost before he could stand. Sidonius Apollinarus, an aristocrat from Gaul, noted: "You would think that the limbs of the man and the horse were born together, so firmly does the rider always stick to the horse. Other people are carried on horseback; these people live there."[7] A Hun horse answered to both bridle and verbal commands, allowing its rider to handle a war bow or other weapon with both hands.

The arms of the Huns were simple, their armor slight. Their primary weapon was the reflex composite bow. Crafted by expert bow-makers out of seven different materials—chiefly wood, bone, and sinew—it measured five feet (1.5 meters) or more in length. Unstrung, the bow curved outward. It could effectively loft an arrow 200 to 300 yards (183 to 274 meters). Arrows were made of wood or reed. The archer carried them in a quiver slung from his belt or saddle.

Hun warriors sometimes used a lasso to thin out enemy formations, roping their foes and dragging them off. They also effectively wielded short, curved swords, daggers, maces, and pickaxes. On rare occasions, they used thrusting and jabbing lances. Small, round shields made of wood and covered with leather completed the Hun's equipment.

Protective clothing consisted of a leather-covered conical helmet, chain mail around the neck and shoulders, and body armor of hard leather greased with animal fat for waterproofing. Hunnic warriors usually wore baggy goatskin pants and soft boots. Huns protected their horses with face masks and body armor of hardened-leather lamellar (thin plates). Firepower and speed provided the best protection for both Hun and horse.

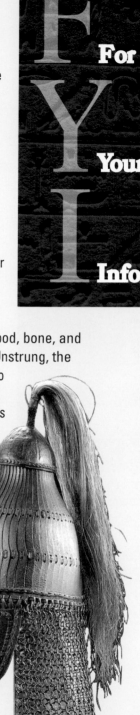

A Hun composite bow (left) and conical helmet

Cameras did not exist in Attila's time, and he was not known to sit for any artist's portraits. Images of the Hun leader rely in part on historical records for his likeness and not a little on the imagination of his portrayer.

CHAPTER

THREE

ZENITH

History has regarded Bleda's death dismissively. Scholars generally credit Attila with his assassination. If Attila was indeed subordinate to his brother, he certainly would have had good cause to remove the only obstacle to his becoming king of the Huns. "A man of Attila's commanding personality," noted Patrick Howarth, one of his biographers, "would not have relished remaining a second-in-command indefinitely."[1] Yet the how of Bleda's passing remains unknown and highly speculative.

Attila biographer John Man advances the theory of a possible coup: "It would have been sudden, brief, and bloody. Bleda vanished from history."[2] No matter the manner of Bleda's death, Attila took sole command of a realm that then stretched from Budapest to the Black Sea and covered an area of almost 200,000 square miles (321,860 square kilometers). Despite the vastness of his empire, Attila did not wait long to expand it further. In 447, he led his Huns into the Eastern Roman Empire for a third time.

Attila could not read or write, but he was a man of rare intelligence. His unifying influence stands as perhaps his greatest achievement. He brought all the Huns together under a centralized authority—himself. His aggressions were aimed not only at conquering the world, but also at keeping his warrior-subjects contented. The spoils of war represented the core of the Hunnic economy. Attila recognized the need to maintain a near-constant state of warfare to sustain the flow of booty. When his warriors started to grumble discontentedly, or his economy showed signs of weakening, he launched a new campaign.

Attila focused his next attack against the East Romans on the provinces of Lower Scythia, Moesia, and Thrace in southeastern Europe. He followed a route that took him farther to the east of his previous campaign. His army moved slower and inflicted greater destruction than before, moving relentlessly toward its goal of Constantinople. Attila bypassed new Roman fortifications along the way and detoured here and there to pillage various cities. Notable among the razed cities were Singidunum (Belgrade), Naissus (Nis), Serdica (Sofia), and Adrianople (Edirne). Callinicus, a monk living near the East Roman capital, described the horrors of Attila's destructive advance about twenty years later:

> The barbarian people of the Huns, the ones in Thrace, became so strong that they captured more than 100 cities, and almost brought Constantinople into danger, and most men fled from it. Even the monks wanted to run away to Jerusalem. There was so much killing and blood-letting that no one could number the dead. They pillaged the churches and monasteries, and slew the monks and virgins. . . . They so devastated Thrace that it will never rise again.[3]

Callinicus's chilling description of Attila's advance probably did little to lessen the Hunnic leader's fearsome reputation as the "Scourge of God" (*Flagellum Dei* in Latin). The phrase—said to be self-imposed by Attila—derives from an ancient Roman type of whip called a scourge. The whip was designed to inflict the maximum amount of harm and pain upon the victim. Attila saw himself as an instrument of a higher power, appointed to punish those unworthy in the eyes of his heathen god. Constantinople, it appears, had to cope with much more than a scourge.

After the Huns withdrew from Gallipoli, probably in 445, a series of natural and human-made disasters befell Constantinople. Bloody riots among horse- and chariot-racing factions erupted in the Hippodrome (stadium), followed by a plague and a famine in 445. After a second plague in 446, a four-month series of earthquakes leveled much of the

Woe be to those who stood in the path of Attila and his invading hordes. In the spring of 452, after being repulsed by Aetius in the Battle of Châlons, Attila snapped back quickly. He passed through the Alps and launched an invasion deep into Italy. The Adriatic fortress-town of Aquileia was the first to feel his wrath.

capital. Thousands of residents were killed, and a third epidemic broke out. The last temblor struck on the morning of January 26, 447, just as Attila rode south into Moesia.

News of Attila's latest incursion soon reached Constantinople. The earthquakes had left gaping holes in the walls of the city and destroyed fifty-seven towers. Panic set in among the ruins of the exposed capital. City official Flavius Constantinus directed a remarkable reconstruction effort and restored the capital's defenses in just two months. If Attila had attacked swiftly, as the Huns usually did, he might have captured the city. That did not happen. Instead, he chose to move slowly to maximize his plunder along the way.

Even with its walls repaired, Constantinople remained at risk. Popular confidence in Flavius Zeno, the commander responsible for the city's defense, waned. Citizens began to flee the capital. Theodosius II appointed a new commander, a German named Arnegliscus. Rather than wait to fight Attila at the walls of the city, Arnegliscus sallied forth with a large army and met the Huns at the Utus (Vid) River. His impatience reaped the reward of a disastrous defeat at the hands of Attila's Huns. But Attila suffered serious battle losses of his own. Disease claimed many more of his marauders. He abandoned his drive on Constantinople to regroup. The city survived again.

When his army recovered, Attila laid waste to the Balkan provinces. He destroyed no less than seventy cities, including Marcianople, the largest city in Thrace. Attila then drove southward into Greece. Forces of the Eastern Empire finally stopped him at Thermopylae (thur-MOP-uh-lee). Theodosius II again sued for peace with the Huns, and the two factions engaged in negotiations over the next three years.

Later in 447, representatives of Theodosius reached an agreement with Attila in the Second Peace of Anatolius. The East Romans agreed to continue an unknown amount of annual tribute to the Huns. They also agreed to evacuate a strip of territory south of the Danube. This buffer zone between the Hunnic and Eastern Roman Empires measured 100 miles (161 kilometers) in width and stretched 300 miles (483 kilometers) eastward from modern Belgrade. Peace prevailed for a time, but Attila continued to press his demands. Theodosius at last realized that there could be no lasting peace with the Huns as long as Attila existed. An assassination plot took root in the emperor's mind.

In 449, Attila sent Edecon (EE-duh-kon) and Orestes (or-EST-eez), two of his top lieutenants, to Constantinople. Their mission was to resolve ongoing differences with the East Romans. When Attila's envoys arrived in the East Roman capital, Chrysaphius (kri-SAY-fee-us), an adviser to the emperor, approached Edecon (also Edika) with a proposition to slay Attila. Also, said Chrysaphius, Edecon might expect to be "the lord of a golden-roofed house and of such wealth [as the emperor's] if he would disregard [Hunnic] matters and take up Roman ways."[4] Edecon agreed to murder his master for fifty pounds of gold and promises of future titles and riches. He wanted the gold to ensure the cooperation of selected accomplices. An interpreter named Bigilas (BIG-uh-lus) was to deliver it during the second stage of negotiations with Attila.

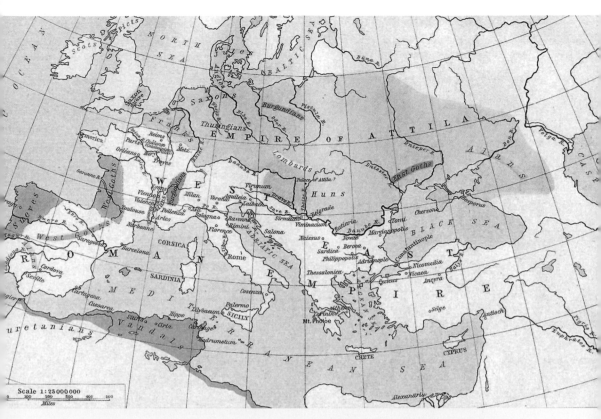

About 450 CE, Attila's Hunnic empire stretched from the Steppes of Central Asia in the east to deep into modern-day Germany in the west, and from the Baltic Sea in the north to the Black Sea in the south.

The emperor's diplomatic party, headed by his ambassador Maximinus and Greek historian Priscus, set out from Constantinople in the early summer of 449. Bigilas, who was carrying the gold, went along as a minor official. Edecon and Orestes and their party returned separately by a different route. When the East Roman party arrived at Attila's home quarters near the river Tisza in Hungary, Attila invited the envoys to an afternoon banquet. The host opened the feasting with a round of toasts. Priscus found himself fascinated by the contrast between the provisions made for the guests and the other Huns and those made for Attila himself.

"A luxurious meal, served on silver plate, had been made ready for us and the barbarian guests," Priscus wrote later, "but Attila ate nothing but meat on a wooden trencher [platter]. In everything else, too, he showed himself temperate; his cup was of wood, while to the guests were given goblets of gold and silver."[5] Priscus also seemed captivated by his host's frugal appearance. "His dress, too, was quite simple, affecting only to be clean. The sword he carried at his side, the lachets of his [Hunnic] shoes, the bridle of his horse were not adorned, like those of the other [Huns], with gold or gems or anything costly."[6] Priscus went on at length to describe Attila's hospitality. Meanwhile, the plot to slay Attila took an unpredictable turn.

Attila's disdainful glare cut the air like the sharp blade at his side.

Somewhere along the way, Edecon had undergone a change of heart. Upon his arrival at Attila's camp, he revealed the details of the impending assassination attempt to his master. When Bigilas arrived with the gold, the Huns seized and chained him. Attila sent the gold back to Theodosius with a taunting message. Noting that they were both sons of nobility, he declared: "I have preserved my noble lineage, but Theodosius has not. Who now is the barbarian, and who the more civilized?"[7]

Theodosius, embarrassed to no end by Attila's discovery of the plot, decided to come clean about his role in it. To make amends, he signed the Third Peace of Anatolius, which restored peace, annual tributes to the Huns, and the return of their defectors.

By 450 CE, Attila had led his Huns to the zenith of their empire and exhausted the wealth of the East Romans. But his plundering followers kept demanding more. Attila turned his eyes to the west, where he hoped to find a new source of riches.

Fighting Tactics of the Huns

Rapid movement—both on the way to battle and in its flow—represented the key element in the Hunnic style of fighting. Hun horsemen were the premier cavalry of their age. Lacking infantry and heavy siege equipment, they relied on lightning-fast maneuvers to surprise and defeat their enemies. Huns operated out of the great Hungarian plains, but no one within thousands of miles felt safe. They ranged so far and so fast that unsuspecting city garrisons fell before their onslaughts almost before they knew what was happening.

The horse provided swift mobility for the Huns. Each Hunnic warrior had at least one spare mount; some had as many as seven remounts. They were saddled and equipped with extra quivers and standard rations. Each horse constituted a self-contained logistical unit. Chariot-like carts drawn by two or three horses lent added support to their movements. Huns could travel several thousand miles without the need of an operational support base.

Over time, the Huns absorbed many of their enemies into their armies—Goths, Gepids, and others. Many of these former enemies fought dismounted as infantry. Huns generally shunned hand-to-hand combat. They preferred to use their bows from a distance for several reasons. Hunnic armor effectively protected them and their horses against arrows but offered little protection against the heavy cut-and-thrust weapons of many of their enemies. At close range, their horses became vulnerable to enemy spears and lances. Most important, because of their small population base, they could ill afford to sustain heavy losses.

At the height of battle, Huns often turned and ran, simulating a retreat to lure their enemy into a trap. If their enemy gave chase in anticipation of a coup, hidden Hun forces would attack from all sides and destroy the confused pursuers.

Mongolian horses (above) share similar physical characteristics with the Steppes-bred horses of the Huns.

Images of Attila varied wildly in the eyes of each beholder. In this artist's conception of him in battle, Attila rides roughshod over the dead and dying. Astride a white charger more appropriate to knights of a later era, he wields a flail and grasps a pair of javelins.

CHAPTER
FOUR

ATTILA VS. AETIUS

Scholars differ as to why Attila suddenly abandoned his activities in the Eastern Empire and looked westward. Hugh Kennedy, a professor of Middle Eastern history, asserts that it was for "reasons that we do not completely understand."[1] Yet speculation as to Attila's reasons abounds. "Most probably he thought the Thracian and Illyrian [east Adriatic coast] provinces were too stripped from earlier raids to be worth ravaging,"[2] suggests historian Erik Hildinger. Biographer and historian John Man concludes, "Within the year his vassals [subordinates], possibly his own *logades* [elites of his power base], would be restless. Something had to be done."[3] Central Asian scholar Stuart Legg agrees:

> [H]is need for a perpetually increasing volume of tribute was imperative. More might be wrung from the eastern empire, but its extraction would be difficult and the returns diminishing. The western empire was still untouched. He made up his mind: he would come to terms with Constantinople, and march into the west.[4]

Quite likely, a dramatic turn of events in Constantinople in 450 had something to do with Attila's decision to come to terms with the Eastern capital and move west. In July of that year, Theodosius II went riding or hunting and was thrown from his horse. He sustained a fatal spinal injury and died on July 28. His sister, Pulcheria, succeeded him as the first Roman empress. She reigned for less than a month, just long enough to order and oversee the execution of the scheming Chrysaphius, her brother's treacherous adviser. Pulcheria then married Marcian, a former professional soldier and an honorary senator of about sixty, and thrust the burden of empire upon him.

"It was the opinion of Marcian," observed Edward Gibbon, "that war should be avoided as long as it is possible to preserve a secure and honourable peace; but it was likewise his opinion that peace cannot be honourable or secure, if the sovereign betrays a pusillanimous [timid or cowardly] aversion to war."[5] Marcian betrayed no such aversion. One of his first acts as sovereign was to cut off the annual tribute in gold that was then being paid to Attila and his Huns. Marcian told the barbarians that he preferred peace but was prepared for war.

Attila put off any action against the resolute Marcian for another day, possibly for the reason stated by biographer Patrick Howarth: "The explanation for Attila's change of policy was, no doubt, that he was already directing his attention to other lands, and for this purpose he wanted stability and peace in his relations with the Eastern Empire."[6] At this point, all Attila needed to invade the Western Empire was a good excuse. It came in an unexpected way.

In 450 CE, Valentinian III ruled as the titular head of the Western Roman Empire from its capital in Ravenna, Italy. He was the son of Constantius III and Galla Placidia. Until his death in 421, Contantius ruled briefly as co-emperor with Honorius. When Honorius died in 423, John the Usurper ruled until he was deposed two years later. Galla Placidia controlled the empire as regent in her son's name until he came of age in 437.

Valentinian III spent much of his reign in pursuit of personal pleasure. While he frolicked and dissipated in Ravenna and thereabouts, Aetius controlled the government from Gaul. Aetius, it might be recalled, was the Roman general who had lived among the Huns and had once aided Ruga, Attila's predecessor. He had risen from the rank of *magister utriusque militiae* ("master of both services," that is, infantry and cavalry) to be given the title of patrician (aristocrat) in 435. His high station would soon put him at odds with the latest aims of Attila. The intrigues of the emperor's sister, Honoria, would hasten and abet the inevitable clash between the two leaders.

Honoria was something of a free spirit, brazen enough to carry on an affair with her steward. Discovery of her illicit romance created a royal scandal. Gossip of her misconduct traveled as far as Constantinople. Regal punishment was swift and severe. Valentinian forcibly betrothed his sister to an elderly senator and executed her steward. Honoria frowned, to say the least, on this unhappy arrangement and reacted with imagination. She sent another of her personal assistants to Attila with a ring and a message: "Be my defender!"[7]

Attila interpreted the receipt of Honoria's ring and plea as a marriage proposal. He pretended to accept her offer and promptly demanded half of the Western Empire as her dowry. Valentinian, of course, refused. He ordered the messenger beheaded and turned his sister over to the care of her resolute mother, Galla Placidia. Honoria was not heard of again. But Attila now had an excuse to invade the Western Roman Empire. Under the guise of claiming his bride and pursuing her dowry, Attila launched his most famous campaign in the spring of 451.

Attila moved up the Danube with an army of tens of thousands. It consisted of all available Huns and included allied subject peoples— Ostrogoths, Rugi, Heruli, Gepids, and others. Most of his allies were of Germanic extraction. When his army reached the Rhine River, he picked up a large body of Franks. Jordanes exaggerated the size of his combined forces at a half-million strong. Attila crossed the Rhine near Coblenz (Koblenz, Germany). Dividing his army into three columns, he swung to the left and spread terror and destruction across Gaul (France).

Almost every major population center between the Rhine and the Seine fell before the onslaught of Attila's barbarian horsemen. One by one, they stripped cities of their treasures and burned them to the ground.

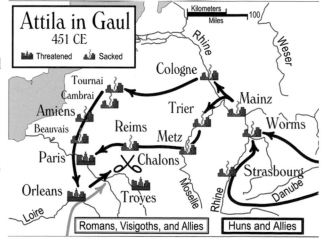

Attila in Gaul
451 CE
🏰 Threatened   🏰 Sacked

Romans, Visigoths, and Allies   Huns and Allies

Their destruction of Metz, as described by Gregory of Tours, set the tone for what was to come: "[T]he Huns, issuing from Pannonia [now Hungary], reached the town of Metz on the vigil of the feast of Easter, devastating the whole country. They gave the city to the flames and slew the people with the edge of the sword, and did to death the priests of the Lord before the holy altars."[8] They went on to strip and torch Cambrai, Arras, Amiens, Reims, and Beauvais in similar fashion.

While Attila's minions were ravaging northern Gaul, Aetius hustled about in the south to put together a defense. As a patrician and senior official of the West Roman government, part of his duties was to prevent refugee Germanic tribes from acquiring too firm a grip in Gaul. One such tribe was the Visigoths led by their aging king, Theodoric II. The Visigoths had fled before the Hun advance a half century earlier and had settled in Toulouse. In discharging his duties, Aetius had made enemies of the Visigoths and their king. Somehow, under the threat of Attila's advance, Aetius managed to strike an alliance with Theodoric and his Visigothic army. With Attila rapidly bearing down upon Orléans, 70 miles (113 kilometers) south of Paris, the newly allied armies of Aetius and Theodoric rushed north to give him battle.

Aetius and his allies arrived at Orléans just as Attila's hordes were entering the town on June 14. They engaged the Huns, who seemed to be losing their momentum, and forced Attila to retire to the east. Attila wanted no part of hand-to-hand combat in the confining quarters of the town. Aetius and Theodoric gave chase and caught up with him at an open area near present-day Châlons-sur-Marne (shah-LOHN-soor-MARN). The region, which is located 95 miles (153 kilometers) east of Paris, is known as the Catalaunian (kat-uh-LAW-nee-an) Plains. Historians recall its fields as the site of Attila's first and only defeat. In the gently contoured country of Champagne, Attila turned to face Aetius in an open ground more favorable to his rapidly mobile style of fighting.

On June 20, 451, East and West clashed in a frantic medley of thundering hooves, clanking blades, and shrieking humanity. The two armies fought all day long. That night, Attila braced for Aetius's second attack. It never came. Aetius left the battlefield the next day and persuaded his allies to do the same. Attila led his Huns to the east—bloodied and humbled, but far from down and out. In 452, he invaded Italy.

Battle of Châlons

"I shall hurl the first spear at the foe," Attila declared before the battle. "If any man can stand at rest while Attila fights, he is a dead man."[9] Goth historian Jordanes recorded this grim admonition as Attila's last words to his Hun cavalry before engaging the armies of Aetius and Theodoric II.

Many historians rank the Battle of Châlons—also referred to as the Battle of the Catalaunian Plains—as one of history's most decisive battles. Scholars generally place its unsure setting in the Champagne area, south of Châlons-sur-Marne. They most often cite the date of the battle as June 20, 451. Some place it as late as September 27. Estimates of the numbers of combatants vary widely. Attila probably fielded about 30,000 cavalry and was likely greatly outnumbered.

"There was [an] unyielding and long-drawn-out battle,"[10] wrote Jordanes. Visigoths led by Thorismond, the son of Goth king Theodoric II, quickly occupied the high ground overlooking Attila's left flank. Attila's horsemen answered by smashing through an Alani contingent manning the center of the Goth-Roman formation. Wheeling to their left, the Huns fell upon the Visigoths. A wild

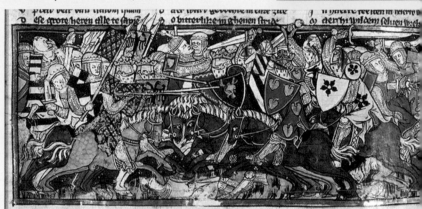

An illustration from an illuminate manuscript depicts the Battle of the Catalaunian Plains (Châlons).

melee ensued. Theodoric was killed in the fighting, but Thorismond rallied the Goths and drove the Huns from the field in a counterattack. Farther east, Attila formed a defensive circle with supply wagons and waited for the next day's attack. The second attack—preempted by Roman politics—never came.

Aetius had long been a friend to the Huns. He understood that their extermination would leave him potentially vulnerable to the victorious Visigoths. The best interests of the Western Roman Empire, he believed, would be better served by maintaining a balance of power among the barbarians. He let the Huns withdraw to the east. The Battle of Châlons ended in a virtual draw, but it thwarted Attila's attempt to extend his empire to the sea.

After the death of Visigoth leader Theodoric II in the Battle of Châlons, his forces rallied under the leadership of his son, Thorismond. At the end of the day's fighting, the Visigoths lifted him upon his shield on the battlefield and hailed him as their new king.

CHAPTER
FIVE

"MOURNED . . .
WITH THE BLOOD OF MEN"

After the bloody clash with the Romans and Goths on the Catalaunian Plains, Attila's Huns limped back to their Hungarian heartland. Most historians credit Aetius with saving Gaul in a great victory. It is true that he turned back the Huns in their drive across the Western Empire. It is also true that Attila absorbed heavy losses in the fray. But so, too, did Aetius. And Theodoric II paid with his life. The actual fighting ended in pretty much of a standoff. Any victory ascribed to Aetius resulted more from the battle's strategic implications than from Western heroics on the battlefield.

Some historians believe that the battle's significance lay mostly in the extent to which it influenced the shape of an emerging Europe. For example, had Attila won a clear victory, the Germanic and Christian empire founded by Charlemagne might not have evolved as it did. It succeeded the Roman Empire, they say, largely because Aetius turned back Attila and his Huns. However, this opinion holds true only if assuming that Attila intended to add Western Europe to his Hunnic Empire. Other scholars think that he invaded the West only as a new source of plunder, with no intention of occupying it. His true intention will probably never be known. Rather, it must be judged solely by what he did next.

"Neither the spirit, nor the forces, nor the reputation of Attila were impaired by the failure of the Gallic expedition," noted Edward Gibbon in *The Decline and Fall of the Roman Empire.* "In the ensuing spring [of 452] he repeated his demand of the princess Honoria and her patrimonial treasures [dowry]."[1] Gibbon referred to Attila's invasion of the West as an *expedition.* He may or may not have used the term as an indication of how he viewed Attila's intention. (*Expedition* does not imply seizure or occupancy of land.) In any case, Attila continued to do what he did best: raid and plunder. "[Attila's] demand was again rejected or eluded," continued Gibbon, "and the indignant lover immediately took the field, passed the Alps, invaded Italy, and besieged Aquileia [ah-kwee-LAY-yah] with an innumerable host of barbarians."[2]

Attila used the pursuit of Honoria's hand and dowry as his excuse to invade Italy, but Honoria had already fallen through the cracks of unrecorded history. He doubtlessly had other reasons as well, not the least of which was the Hunnic economy that lived on ill-gotten gains. And— despite Gibbon's assessment of Attila's reputation—there was also the question of his damaged image. "Attila was furious about the unexpected defeat suffered in Gaul," scribed Hydatius, a fifth-century Spanish chronicler, "and he turned to Italy in his rage."[3]

Aquileia, the first city to feel Attila's rage, held out for about three months. It was a fortress-town on the Adriatic coast, with a proud history of defending Italy's northeast corner. His warriors were beginning to grumble over the long siege. Attila was about to lift the siege and bypass the city when he noticed storks leaving the city. According to Jordanes, quoting Priscus, Attila told his men: "Look at the birds, which foresee what is to come, leaving the doomed city, deserting endangered strongholds which are about to fall."[4] The Huns took heart, broke out the battering rams, and breached the city's walls.

Attila and his Huns vented their pent-up rage against the city, which, in the words of Jordanes, "they despoiled, smashed asunder and devastated so savagely that they left hardly a trace of it to be seen."[5] They went on to ravage a half-dozen smaller towns. Notable among them were Concordia and Altinum. Rather than suffer similar destruction, another half-dozen cities along the edge of the Po valley opened their gates to the mercies of the barbarians. Padua, Vicenza, Verona, Brescia, Bergamo, and Milan all fell victim to the invaders. Many refugees from Attila's killing

On their drive into the Italian peninsula, the invading Huns savagely ravaged and destroyed all the cities in their path. Terror and death rode with them.

fields fled to the clustered offshore Gulf islands from which later rose the fabled city of Venice.

Aetius, despite an army weakened by the Châlons affair, remained firm in his will to resist the approaching Huns. Valentinian III fled Ravenna for Rome; some say out of cowardice, others say out of the need to look for reinforcements. Neither of their wills was tested. Attila, whose ultimate objective was thought to have been Rome itself, never crossed the Appenines for several obscure reasons. Disease played a role. Dysentery and malaria thinned the ranks of his Huns. Drought claimed more Huns through starvation. At the same time, Marcian sent East Roman troops across the Danube, possibly giving Attila reason to back off. Priscus suggested that Attila also feared he might suffer the fate of the Visigoth leader Alaric, who died soon after sacking Rome in 410.

Prosper of Aquitaine, a contemporary chronicler, offered a further explanation. A diplomatic mission headed by Pope Leo I the Great and including the prefect Trigetus and the consul Aviennus met with Attila on the banks of the Mincio River near Lake Garda. "The king [Attila] received the whole delegation courteously," wrote Prosper, "and he was so flattered by the presence of the highest priest that he ordered his men to stop hostilities and, promising peace, returned beyond the Danube."[6] Attila went home without Honoria or her dowry, but perhaps not entirely

In **The Meeting of Leo the Great with Attila** *(1511–14), a fresco in the Vatican's papal suite, Italian Renaissance painter Raphael depicts Saint Peter and Saint Paul (above) brandishing swords and driving off Attila.*

empty-handed. Some historians, including Isaac Azimov, suggest that Pope Leo brought a large quantity of gold—as well as divine direction— to help persuade the Hun chieftain to abandon his latest expedition.

Probably all of these reasons influenced Attila's decision to return to his home base in the Hungarian heartland. Once home, Attila began to prepare for his next campaign—yet another excursion into the Eastern Roman Empire. While preparations moved forward in the early spring of 453, he somehow found time to take another wife. Hunnic tradition allowed a man to wed as many women as he could afford to support. In Attila's case, this meant as many wives as he wanted. His latest wife was a Gothic maiden named Ildico. After a spirited wedding feast, the newlyweds retired to Attila's bedroom.

Priscus recorded what happened next, but his original account was lost. Jordanes copied it, however, and thus preserved the story of Attila's wedding night:

> He had given himself up to excessive merry-making and he threw
> himself down on his back heavy with wine and sleep. He suffered
> a haemorrhage, and the blood, which would ordinarily have
> drained through his nose, was unable to pass through the usual
> passages and flowed in its deadly course down his throat, killing
> him. This drunkenness brought a shameful end to a king who had
> won glory in war.[7]

The next day, Attila's attendants felt reluctant to disturb him too
early. When he did not appear much later in the day, they suspected that
something was wrong and broke open the door to his bedroom. "There
they found the death of Attila accomplished by an effusion of blood,"
continued the Priscus/Jordanes account, "without any wound, and the girl
with downcast face weeping beneath her veil."[8]

The account originated by Priscus and copied by Jordanes
represents the generally accepted version of Attila's death. During more
than a millennium and a half since his passing, other versions of his death
have surfaced—including assassination theories. But failing the discovery
of additional historical information, Priscus's original account of his
demise will likely remain the most popular version.

When Attila's warriors learned of his death, they cut off their hair
and gashed their faces with their swords. They wished for their great king
to "be mourned with no feminine lamentations and with no tears,"
according to Jordanes, "but with the blood of men."[9] His horsemen
galloped in circles around his body while it lay in state in his silken tent.
Later, they buried their chieftain in a triple coffin of gold, silver, and iron,
along with spoils from his many conquests, somewhere between the
Danube and Tisza rivers on the Great Hungarian Plain.

Attila's grave has never been found. Some say his *logades*—"chosen
few"—slew all the members of the burial party to keep its location secret.
After lamenting and feasting at his gravesite, his horsemen galloped over
his grave to remove all signs of disturbed earth. Overflow waters from the
two great rivers soon removed any remaining traces of their great king's
grave. And so passed Attila, the Scourge of God, whose death was
celebrated by millions but also *"mourned . . . with the blood of men."*

After Attila

Just as Germany's Third Reich would die with the death of Adolf Hitler in the twentieth century, the Hunnic Empire died with Attila. Jordanes summed up its demise in a single sentence: "A contest for the highest place arose among Attila's successors—for the minds of young men are wont to be inflamed by ambition for power—and in their heedless rush to rule, they all destroyed the empire."[10] Attila's sons Ellak, Dengizik, and Ernak squabbled over how to divvy up their father's legacy. Ellak, as eldest son and designated

Attila's eldest son, Ellak

successor, became the next king of the Huns. Dengizik and Ernak satisfied themselves begrudgingly with control of some of the peoples subordinate to the Huns—Ostrogoths, Gepids, and others. (Rule over people rather than over territory reflected a reversion to the earlier ways of their once nomadic race.) Attila would not have long stood for such a division of authority. Witness the death of Bleda. This divided rule soon led to rebellion among the independent tribes.

In 454, Ardaric, leader of the Gepids and once one of Attila's stoutest allies, led a major revolt against Ellak. A great battle took place at the Nedao River in Pannonia. Andaric's followers killed some 30,000 Huns and Hun allies, according to Jordanes. (In light of his tendency to exaggerate, the number of dead probably totaled closer to 3,000.) The slain included Ellak. In 469, Dengizik was killed and beheaded in the East Empire. Ernak's fate remains unknown. Within two decades of Attila's death, the Huns disappeared from earthly view. "Thus did the Huns give way," wrote Jordanes, "a race to which men thought the whole world must yield."[11]

Aetius, Attila's chief rival and dutiful defender of the West, met death by a dozen blades in 454, in a murder plot inspired and instigated by the fear and envy of his ruler, Valentinian III. Two assassins struck Valentinian dead with blows to the head the following year. In the East, Marcian died from disease, possibly gangrene, in 457. His empire endured as the Byzantine Empire through the Middle Ages. Rome fell to German invaders in 476. Attila was perhaps smiling somewhere.

Chapter 1. The Rise of the Huns

1. John Man, *Attila: The Barbarian King Who Challenged Rome* (London: Bantam Press, 2005), p. 35.
2. Ibid., p. 11.
3. Stuart Legg, *The Barbarians of Asia* (New York: Barnes & Noble Books, 1995), p. 140.
4. Edward Gibbon, *The Decline and Fall of the Roman Empire* (Great Books of the Western World. Vols. 40 and 41; Gibbon I and II. Robert Maynard Hutchins, Editor in Chief. Chicago: Encyclopaedia Britannica, 1952), vol. I, p. 417.
5. Erik Hildinger, *Warriors of the Steppes: A Military History of Central Asia, 500 B.C. to 1700 A.D.* (Cambridge, MA: Da Capo Press, 2001), p. 57.
6. Ibid., pp. 57–58.

Chapter 2. And Then There Was One

1. Norman F. Cantor (editor), *The Encyclopedia of the Middle Ages* (New York: Viking, 1999), p. 53.
2. Erik Hildinger, *Warriors of the Steppes: A Military History of Central Asia, 500 B.C. to 1700 A.D.* (Cambridge, MA: Da Capo Press, 2001), p. 58.
3. Michael A. Babcock, *The Night Attila Died: Solving the Murder of Attila the Hun* (New York: Berkley Books, 2005), p. 8.
4. Ibid.
5. John Man, *Attila: The Barbarian King Who Challenged Rome* (London: Bantam Press, 2005), p. 139.
6. Babcock, p. 75.
7. Hugh Kennedy, *Mongols, Huns and Vikings: Nomads at War* (London: Cassell, 2002), p. 29.

Chapter 3. Zenith

1. Patrick Howarth, *Attila, King of the Huns: The Man and the Myth* (New York: Carroll & Graf Publishers, 2001), p. 39.
2. John Man, *Attila: The Barbarian King Who Challenged Rome* (London: Bantam Press, 2005), p. 137.
3. Ibid., p. 150.
4. Howarth, pp. 66–67.
5. Medieval Sourcebook: Priscus at the court of Attila. http://www.fordham.edu/halsall/source/priscus1.html, p. 6.
6. Ibid.
7. Man, p. 190.

Chapter 4. Attila vs. Aetius

1. Hugh Kennedy, *Mongols, Huns and Vikings: Nomads at War* (London: Cassell, 2002), pp. 48, 50.
2. Erik Hildinger, *Warriors of the Steppes: A Military History of Central Asia, 500 B.C. to 1700 A.D.* (Cambridge, MA: Da Capo Press, 2001), p. 68.
3. John Man, *Attila: The Barbarian King Who Challenged Rome* (London: Bantam Press, 2005), p. 193.
4. Stuart Legg, *The Barbarians of Asia* (New York: Barnes & Noble Books, 1995), p. 146.
5. Edward Gibbon, *The Decline and Fall of the Roman Empire* (Great Books of the Western World. Vols. 40 and 41; Gibbon I and II. Robert Maynard Hutchins, Editor in Chief. Chicago: Encyclopaedia Britannica, 1952), vol. I, p. 558.
6. Patrick Howarth, *Attila, King of the Huns: The Man and the Myth* (New York: Carroll & Graf Publishers, 2001), pp. 79–80.
7. Michael A. Babcock, *The Night Attila Died: Solving the Murder of Attila the Hun* (New York: Berkley Books, 2005), p. 150.
8. Howarth, p. 99.
9. Ibid., p. 111.
10. Kennedy, p. 52.

Chapter 5. "Mourned . . . with the Blood of Men"

1. Edward Gibbon, *The Decline and Fall of the Roman Empire* (Great Books of the Western World. Vols. 40 and 41; Gibbon I and II. Robert Maynard Hutchins, Editor in Chief. Chicago: Encyclopaedia Britannica, 1952), vol. I, p. 566.
2. Ibid.
3. Michael A. Babcock, *The Night Attila Died: Solving the Murder of Attila the Hun* (New York: Berkley Books, 2005), p. 221.
4. John Man, Attila: *The Barbarian King Who Challenged Rome* (London: Bantam Press, 2005), p. 251.
5. Ibid., p. 253.
6. Ibid., p. 255.
7. Ibid., p. 262.
8. Babcock, p. 243.
9. The Planets: Attila the Hun http://www.the-planets.com/star-biography/Attila_the_Hun_Biography.htm, p. 4.
10. Man, p. 276.
11. Ibid.

c.406   Attila is born.

429   Aetius, general and chief minister of Valentinian III, becomes *de facto* (actual) ruler of Western Roman Empire until assassinated by Valentinian in 454.

434   Ruga dies; Attila becomes king of the Huns and rules jointly with his elder brother Bleda.

435   Huns sign Treaty of Margus with the Eastern Roman Empire.

441   Attila invades the Eastern Roman Empire.

443   Attila launches second campaign against the Eastern Roman Empire. First Peace of Anatolius is signed.

445   Bleda dies, probably assassinated by his brother; Attila assumes total control over the Huns.

447   Attila unleashes third campaign against the Eastern Romans. Second Peace of Anatolius is signed.

449   Roman plot to murder Attila fails. Third Peace of Anatolius is signed.

450   Eastern Roman Emperor Theodosius II dies. Marcian, successor to Theodosius II, withdraws from treaties with the Huns; terminates annual tributes to them established by the Peace of Anatolius.

451   Attila invades Gaul (France). Aetius repulses Attila on the Catalaunian Plains (Battle of Châlons).

452   Attila mounts campaign into Northern Italy. Venice is founded by refugees from Attila's Huns.

453   Attila marries Ildico and dies on his wedding night, allegedly by choking on his own blood from a nosebleed. Ellak, Attila's eldest son, succeeds him as king of the Huns.

TIMELINE IN HISTORY

350	Christianity reaches Abyssinia (Ethiopia).
360	Huns invade Europe. Picts and Scots cross Hadrian's Wall and attack Britain.
c.360	Books begin to replace scrolls.
364	Roman Empire divides: Eastern half from Lower Danube to Persian border under Valens; Western half from Caledonia to northwestern Africa under Valentinian I.
370	Theodosius drives Picts and Scots out of Britain.
376	Huns invade Russia.
379	Theodosius I becomes coemperor of the Eastern Empire with Gratian.
392	Theodosius I (or Theodosius the Great) accedes as Emperor of East and West, the last ruler of a united Empire. Christianity becomes the official religion of the Roman Empire.
396	After the death of Theodosius I in 395, he is succeeded by Honorius and Arcadius, who redivide the Empire. Alaric, king of the Visigoths, invades Greece.
410	Alaric sacks Rome.
c.410	Medieval chemical science of alchemy begins, focusing mainly on the search for the Philosopher's Stone and the Elixir of Life.
411	St. Augustine writes *City of God* after the sacking of Rome.
425	Constantinople University is founded.
432	St. Patrick embarks on mission to Ireland.
436	Last Roman legions leave Britain.
455	Vandals sack Rome.
470	Huns withdraw from Europe.
c.470	Mayan civilization flourishes in southern Mexico.
476	Western Roman Empire ends; the German barbarian Odoacer deposes Emperor Romulus Augustulus and is proclaimed the first king of Italy.
478	The first Shinto shrines are erected in Japan.
479	Ch'i dynasty founded in southern China.
484	First schism between the Western and the Eastern Churches begins; ends in 519.
493	Theodoric the Great, king of the Ostrogoths, murders Odoacer and founds the Ostrogoth kingdom of Italy.
500	First plans for the Vatican Palace are drafted in Rome.

For Young Adults

Harvey, Bonnie. *Attila the Hun*. Ancient World Leaders Series. New York: Chelsea House Publishers, 2003.

Ingram, W. Scott. *Attila the Hun*. History's Villains Series. Farmington Hills, MI: Gale Group, 2002.

Nicolle, David. *Attila the Hun*. Osprey Trade Editions. New York: Osprey Publishing, 2000.

Oliver, Marilyn Tower. *Attila the Hun*. Heroes and Villains Series. Farmington Hills, MI: Gale Group, 2005.

Vardy, Steven Bela. *Attila*. World Leaders Past and Present Series. New York: Chelsea House Publishers, 1991.

Works Consulted

Babcock, Michael A. *The Night Attila Died: Solving the Murder of Attila the Hun*. New York: Berkley Books, 2005.

Cantor, Norman F. (editor). *The Encyclopedia of the Middle Ages*. New York: Viking, 1999.

Cantor, Norman F. *The Civilization of the Middle Ages*. New York: HarperCollins Publishers, 1993.

Dahmus, Joseph. *A History of the Middle Ages*. New York: Barnes & Noble, 1995.

Davies, Norman. *Europe: A History*. New York: Oxford University Press, 1996.

Dupuy, R. Ernest, and Trevor N. Dupuy. *The Encyclopedia of Military History from 3500 B.C. to the Present*. Revised Edition. New York: Harper & Row, Publishers, 1977.

Durant, Will. *The Age of Faith: A History of Medieval Civilization—Christian, Islamic, and Judaic—from Constantine to Dante: A.D. 325–1300*. New York: Simon and Schuster, 1950.

Gibbon, Edward. *The Decline and Fall of the Roman Empire*. Great Books of the Western World. Vols. 40 and 41; Gibbon I and II. Robert Maynard Hutchins, Editor in Chief. Chicago: Encyclopaedia Britannica, 1952.

Hildinger, Erik. *Warriors of the Steppes: A Military History of Central Asia, 500 B.C. to 1700 A.D.* Cambridge, MA: Da Capo Press, 2001.

Howarth, Patrick. *Attila, King of the Huns: The Man and the Myth*. New York: Carroll & Graf Publishers, 2001.

Kennedy, Hugh. *Mongols, Huns and Vikings: Nomads at War*. London: Cassell, 2002.

Legg, Stuart. *The Barbarians of Asia*. New York: Barnes & Noble Books, 1995.

Man, John. *Attila: The Barbarian King Who Challenged Rome*. London: Bantam Press, 2005.

Nicolle, David. *Attila and the Nomad Hordes*. Osprey Elite Series. New York: Osprey Publishing, 1990.

On the Internet

Medieval Sourcebook: Priscus at the Court of Attila
http://www.fordham.edu/halsall/source/priscus1.html

The Planets: Attila the Hun
http://www.the-planets.com/star-biography/Attila_the_Hun_Biography.htm

GLOSSARY

angon (ahn-ZHAHN)—A barbed lance or javelin used for throwing or for spearing in close quarters.

Flagellum Dei (fluh-JEL-um DAY)—"Scourge of God"; Latin phrase used to describe Attila or the Huns.

depose (dee-POHZ)—To remove from power.

dysentery (DIS-en-tayr-ee)—Inflammation of the intestines causing severe diarrhea.

gangrene (gan-GREEN)—Decay and death of body tissue due to loss of blood supply.

Hippodrome (HIP-puh-drohm)—An oval stadium for horse and chariot racing in ancient Greece.

Hun—A nomadic Central Asian people, possibly descended from the Xiongnu.

Hungnu (HUNG-noo)—Chinese word for "barbarian"; possible source of the name Hun.

logades (loh-GAH-des)—Latin for "chosen few"; elites of Attila's power base.

patrician (puh-TRIH-shun)—A person of high birth: an aristocrat; a member of one of the original citizen families of ancient Rome.

scourge (SKORJ)—An Ancient Roman type of whip designed to inflict the maximum amount of harm and pain upon the victim.

titular (TIH-choo-lar)—Having the title of a ruler without the real authority.

tribute (TRIB-yoot)—Payment that one country or ruler was obliged to pay to a more powerful one.

vassal (VAS-ul)—In feudal times, a subordinate or humble servant.

Xiongnu (shee-OONG-noo)—A Turkic people that menaced China as early as the fifth century BCE; possible forebears of the Huns.

yurt—A circular domed tent of skins or felt stretched over a collapsible lattice framework and used by pastoral peoples of inner Asia; also called a *ger*.

INDEX